W9-BTB-102

Super Simple
Cultural Art

Super Simple
Native AMERICAN ARt

Fun and Easy Art from Around the World

Alex Kuskowski

Consulting Editor, Diane Craig, M.A./Reading Specialist

A Division of ABDO

ABDO
Publishing Company

visit us at www.abdopublishing.com

Published by ABDO Publishing Company, a division of ABDO, P.O. Box 398166, Minneapolis, Minnesota 55439. Copyright © 2012 by Abdo Consulting Group, Inc. International copyrights reserved in all countries. No part of this book may be reproduced in any form without written permission from the publisher. Super SandCastle™ is a trademark and logo of ABDO Publishing Company.

Printed in the United States of America, North Mankato, Minnesota
102011
012012

♻ PRINTED ON RECYCLED PAPER

Editor: Liz Salzmann
Content Developer: Nancy Tuminelly
Interior Design and Production: Oona Gaarder-Juntti, Mighty Media, Inc.
Cover Design: Kelsey Gullickson, Mighty Media, Inc.
Photo Credits: Comstock Images, Jupiterimages, Liquidlibrary, Shutterstock

The following manufacturers/names appearing in this book are trademarks:
Elmer's® Glue-All™, Fiskars®, Glitter Glue™, Lion Brand® Yarn, Scribbles®, Sharpie® Styrofoam™

Library of Congress Cataloging-in-Publication Data

Kuskowski, Alex.
  Super simple native American art : fun and easy art from around the world / Alex Kuskowski.
    p. cm. -- (Super simple cultural art)
  ISBN 978-1-61783-214-7
  1. Indian art--North America--Juvenile literature. 2. Handicraft--North America--Juvenile literature. 3. Indians of North America--Juvenile literature. I. Title.
  TT22.K89 2012
  745.5--dc23
                    2011024603

Super SandCastle™ books are created by a team of professional educators, reading specialists, and content developers around five essential components—phonemic awareness, phonics, vocabulary, text comprehension, and fluency—to assist young readers as they develop reading skills and strategies and increase their general knowledge. All books are written, reviewed, and leveled for guided reading, early reading intervention, and Accelerated Reader® programs for use in shared, guided, and independent reading and writing activities to support a balanced approach to literacy instruction.

TO ADULT HELPERS

Children can have a lot of fun learning about different cultures through arts and crafts. Be sure to supervise them as they work on the projects in this book. Let the kids do as much as possible on their own. But be ready to step in and help if necessary. Also, kids may be using glue, paint, markers, and clay. Make sure they protect their clothes and work surfaces.

Symbols

HOT
You will be working with something hot. Get help.

ADULT HELPER
Ask for help. You will need help from an adult.

Table of Contents

Kachina Dolls

Kachina dolls come from the **Pueblo culture**. The dolls are given to children during special dance ceremonies.

Art Around the World

People from around the world do things differently. That's because of their **culture**. Everyone belongs to a culture, even you! Learning about different cultures can be a lot of fun.

Each culture has its own way of doing things. Often the things the people make show a certain style. Try some of the art projects in this book. See what you can learn about Native American culture! You can even share what you learn with others.

Before You Start

Remember to treat other people and **cultures** with respect. Respect their art, **jewelry**, and clothes too. These things can have special meaning to people.

There are a few rules for doing art projects.

- **Permission**

  Make sure to ask permission to do a project. You might want to use things you find around the house. Ask first!

- **Safety**

  Get help from an adult when using something hot or sharp. Never use an oven by yourself.

Coil Pot

Southwest Indians make **coil** pots. The pots hold food and water.

Art in Native American Culture

Native Americans create many beautiful things. Some are for everyday use. Others are for special occasions. The **designs** in Native American art often have special meanings.

Totem Pole

Native people in the Northwest **carve** totem poles. They are made from tall trees. Some totem poles tell stories. Others honor dead family members.

Medicine Bag

Northern Tribes make medicine bags. They put magical objects in the bags. Medicine bags are usually worn by medicine men.

Headdress

For Native Americans, a headdress is not just for show. Each decoration or feather has a special meaning. Some are for bravery in battle. Others are for helping the community.

Dream Catcher

Dream catchers are made by the **Ojibwe** people. Dream catchers look like spider's webs. Dream catchers are believed to catch bad dreams. They let only good dreams through.

Materials

Here are some of the materials you'll need to get started.

ruler

pony beads

decorative gems

unpopped popcorn

pencil

colored craft sand

dried beans

rice

paper towel tubes

colored string

googly eyes

styrofoam balls

toilet paper tube

polymer clay

foam shapes

8  feathers

newspaper

aluminum foil

construction paper

markers

felt

glue

cardboard

yarn

glitter glue

scissors

acrylic paint

small bowl

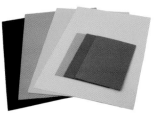
tape

foam sheets

paintbrushes

puffy paint

9

craft ring

hole punch

FEATHERY HEADDRESS

Make a headdress that shows how brave and helpful you are!

WHAT YOU NEED
- ruler
- scissors
- sheets of foam
- construction paper
- glue
- feathers
- hole punch
- yarn

Cut a piece of foam. It should be 2 inches (5 cm) by 18 inches (46 cm). This is the headband.

 Cut out different shapes. Use foam or construction paper. Glue the shapes to the headband. Let the glue dry.

 Turn the headband over. Glue feathers along the top of the headband. Let the glue dry.

Punch a hole in each end of the headband. Cut two pieces of yarn. They should be 12 inches (30 cm) long. Tie one piece of yarn to each hole. Use the yarn to tie the headdress around your head.

11

MUSICAL RAINSTICK

Use your rainstick to try to make it rain or just to make music!

1. Put the bowl upside down on the paper. Trace around it. Put the bowl on another piece of paper. Trace around it again.

2. Put the paper towel tube in the center of a circle. Trace around it. Put it in the other circle. Trace around it again. Draw lines from the small circles to the large circles. Draw about eight lines in each circle.

3. Cut out the two large circles. Then cut along the lines. This makes tabs.

4. Paint the paper towel tube. Let the paint dry.

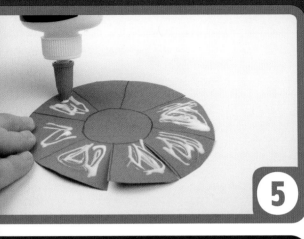

 Put glue on the tabs of one of the circles.

 Place the circle over one end of the tube. Press the tabs down around the tube. This seals the end of the tube.

 Make two twisted pieces of aluminum foil. They should be as long as the tube. Put them inside the tube.

Put some dried beans in the tube.

 Put some rice in the tube.

 Put some unpopped popcorn in the tube.

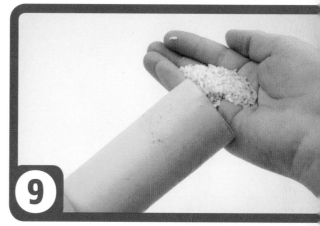

 Glue the second circle over the other end of the tube. Make sure nothing can get out.

 Decorate the tube. Use glitter glue, markers, paint, gems, or craft foam shapes.

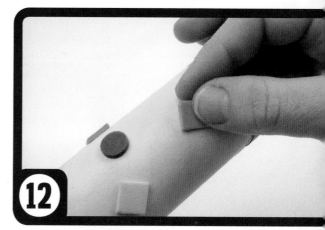

DREAM CATCHER

Make a dream catcher to bring sweet dreams!

16

1 Cut a piece of cardboard. It should be about 2 inches (5 cm) by 3 inches (8 cm). Make a short cut in one end. This is a yarn shuttle.

2 Put one end of the yarn into the cut. Wrap a bunch of yarn around the shuttle. You can add more yarn later. Just tie the ends together. Then wrap more yarn around the shuttle.

3 Tie the other end of the yarn around the craft ring. Tape the end of the yarn to the ring.

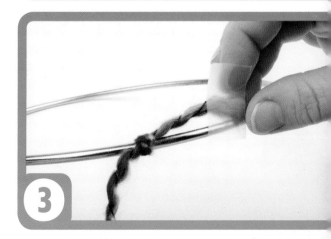

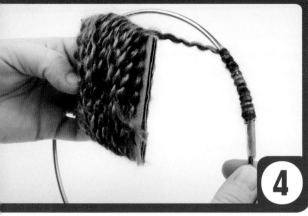

4 Use the shuttle to wrap the yarn around the ring. Wrap it tightly. Cover the entire ring. Tie a couple of knots at the end. Glue the end down.

5 Cut a piece of string. It should be about 10 feet (3 m) long. Tie the string to the ring. Leave about 6 inches (15 cm) at the end of the string.

6 Take the long end of the string. Bring it across the ring. Wrap it twice around the ring. Keep the string tight.

7 Continue wrapping the string around the ring. Go back and forth across the ring. Stop before the final wrap. Put a bead on the string. Then make the final wrap. Tie the string to the ring. Cut off the extra string. Glue the end of the string down.

18

8 Tie the end of the short string around a web string. This makes a **loop**. Use it to hang your dream catcher.

9 Cut a piece of yarn. It should be about 12 inches (30 cm) long. Tie it to the ring. Put it across from the loop. Tie it so the knot is in the middle of the yarn. The ends should be even.

10 Wet the ends of the yarn. Twist them together into a point. Put some beads on the yarn.

11 Tie the ends of the yarn around a feather. Cut off the extra yarn.

12 Stick the end of the feather into the last bead. Repeat steps 9 through 12. Add more strings of beads and feathers.

COOL COIL POT

What will you keep in your coil pot?

WHAT YOU NEED
• polymer clay
• plastic spoon

20

Press the polymer clay with your hands. Keep pressing until it is soft. Roll the clay into a long snake. It should be about as thick as a pencil.

 Wrap one end of the clay into a tight circle. This is the bottom of the pot. Then wind the clay up the sides.

 Gently press the **coils** together. This forms the sides of the pot. You can add different colors if you like.

 Decorate the sides of the pot. Use the edge of a spoon to make lines around the rim.

5 Ask an adult to bake your pot in the oven. Follow the directions that came with the clay.

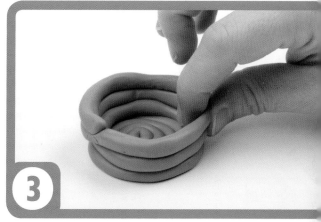

21

MEDICINE BAG

Carry your magical things in your own medicine bag!

1. Cut two pieces of felt. Make them 5 inches (13 cm) square. Draw a line 2 inches (5 cm) in from one side. Make cuts from the edge to the line. This makes **fringe**. Do the same thing with the second piece of felt.

2. Lay one piece of felt down. The pencil line should face up. Put glue on the sides and above the fringe. Press the second piece on top. Let the glue dry.

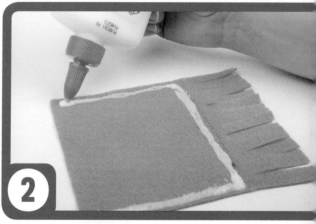

3. Decorate your bag. Draw **designs** with puffy paint. Glue on felt animals.

4. Punch holes in the top corners of the bag. Cut a piece of yarn. It should be 12 inches (30 cm) long. Tie the end to one hole. Put beads on the yarn. Tie the other end of the yarn to the other hole.

TOTEM POLE

Make a totem pole for your family or a special event.

WHAT YOU NEED
- paper towel tube
- ruler
- markers
- acrylic paint
- paintbrush
- glue
- googly eyes
- construction paper
- scissors
- foam shapes
- feathers

Make four marks on the paper towel tube. Make them 2 inches (5 cm) apart. Draw a line around the tube at each mark. Now the tube has five parts. Paint each part a different color. Let the paint dry.

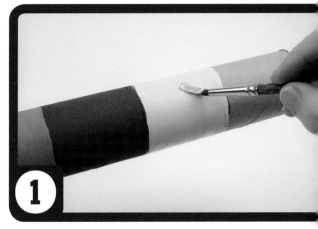

2 Glue googly eyes in each part. Hold them in place until the glue dries.

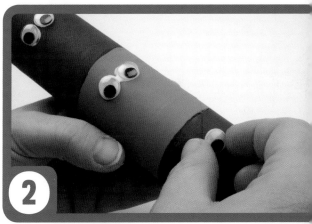

3 Cut four thin strips of construction paper. Glue them around the tube between the parts.

 Make a different face in each part. Use foam shapes, markers, and paint. Cut out some wings. Use foam or construction paper. Glue them to the back of the tube.

5 Glue feathers to the inside of the top of the tube.

25

KACHINA DOLL

Make your own kachina doll and catch dance fever!

WHAT YOU NEED
- toilet paper tube
- Styrofoam ball
- glue
- acrylic paint
- paintbrush
- construction paper
- scissors
- ruler
- marker
- felt
- yarn
- puffy paint
- feathers

26

Glue the Styrofoam ball to one end of the tube. Let the glue dry. This is the doll's head.

 Paint the body and head. Let the paint dry.

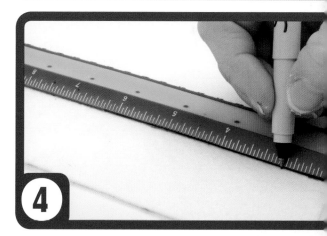 Find pictures of kachina dolls online. Use them to get ideas for your doll. Cut out paper shapes for the face. Glue them on the head.

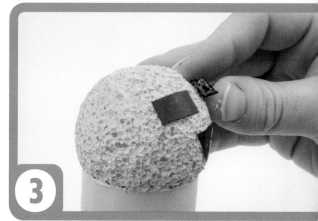 Cut out a strip of felt. It should be 2 inches (5 cm) by 6 inches (15 cm). This is the doll's skirt.

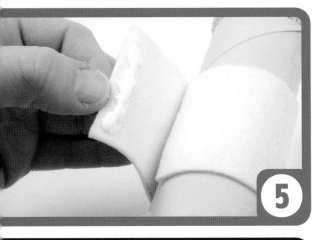

5 Glue one end of the skirt to the tube. Wrap the skirt around the tube. Glue the other end. Make sure the ends are in the back.

6 Cut a thin strip of felt. This is the belt. Glue it around the top of the skirt.

7 Cut a piece of yarn. It should be 6 inches (15 cm) long. Wrap it above the belt. Tie a knot in front. Tie a second piece of yarn around the knot. Cut the ends of the yarn. They should all be the same length.

8 Decorate your doll with puffy paint. Make **designs** on the skirt and on the body.

9 Make a headdress. Poke the ends of the feathers into the Styrofoam head.

SUPER SAND PAINTING

Make a sand painting to keep evil spirits away.

WHAT YOU NEED
- cardboard
- marker
- ruler
- newspaper
- glue
- paintbrushes
- colored craft sand
- plastic spoon

29

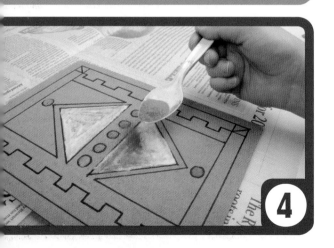

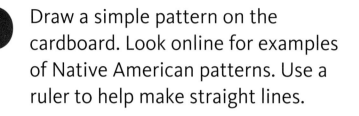

1 Draw a simple pattern on the cardboard. Look online for examples of Native American patterns. Use a ruler to help make straight lines.

2 Cover the table with newspaper. Put the cardboard on the newspaper.

3 Add the sand one color at a time. Dip a paintbrush into the glue. Paint the glue where you want to put the first color. Fill in the areas completely. Don't put the glue on too thick.

4 Use a spoon to pick up some sand. Sprinkle the sand over the wet glue. Cover all of the glued areas.

5 Gently press the sand with your finger. Let the glue dry.

6 Tip the cardboard on its side. Tap the back gently. The loose sand will fall onto the newspaper.

7 Check to see if the glue is covered completely. Use the brush to dab glue onto any missed spots. Then repeat steps 4 through 6.

8 When you are done with one color of sand, save the extra. Move everything off the newspaper. Fold the newspaper. Raise the sides. The sand will go into the fold. Tip the paper. Pour the sand into its bag.

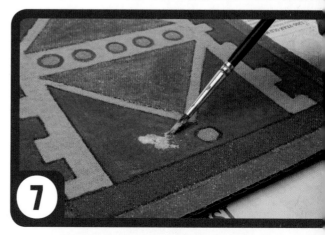

9 Follow steps 3 through 8 for each of the colors in your sand painting.

Conclusion

Did you learn about Native American **culture**? Did you have fun making these art projects? Learning about other cultures is very interesting. You can learn about how people around the world live. Try looking up more **information** about Native Americans!

Glossary

carve – to cut shapes or designs out of something such as wood or stone.

coil – 1. a spiral or a series of circles. 2. one of the circles in a spiral.

culture – the ideas, traditions, art, and behaviors of a group of people.

design – a decorative pattern or arrangement.

fringe – a border made up of hanging strips or threads.

information – the facts known about an event or subject.

jewelry – pretty things, such as rings, necklaces, and bracelets, that you wear for decoration.

loop – a circle made by a rope, string, or thread.

Ojibwe – one of the largest groups of Native Americans. They live in the northern United States and southern Canada.

Pueblo – any of several Native American groups in Arizona and New Mexico.